MEDIEVAL LIVES

Moira Butterfield

Smart Apple Media

Smart Apple Media is published by Black Rabbit Books
P.O. Box 3263, Mankato, Minnesota 56002

Printed in the United States

Published by arrangement with the Watts Publishing Group Ltd, London.

Library of Congress Cataloging-in-Publication Data

Butterfield, Moira, 1961–
    Knight / Moira Butterfield.
    p. cm.—(Smart apple media. Medieval lives)
    Includes bibliographical references and index.
    Summary: "Traces the life of a typical knight in medieval times from birth to death, including childhood,
becoming a knight, going to war, pilgrimages, and knightly duties. Includes primary source quotes"—
Provided by publisher.
    ISBN 978-1-59920-168-9
    1. Knights and knighthood—Juvenile literature. 2. Civilization, Medieval—Juvenile literature. I. Title.
CR4513.B84 2009
940.1—dc22
                                                                            2007050616

Artwork: Gillian Clements
Editor: Sarah Ridley
Editor in chief: John C. Miles
Designer: Simon Borrough
Art director: Jonathan Hair
Picture research: Diana Morris

Picture credits:
ArquBiblioteca d'Ajuda Lisbon/ Gianni Dagli Orti/The Art Archive: 11. Biblioteca Monasterio del Escorial Madrid/Bridgeman Art
Library:36. Biblioteca Nazionale Marciana Venice/Alfredo Dagli Orti/The Art Archive: 19. Biblioteca Nazionale Marciana
Venice/Gianni Dagli Orti/The Art Archive: 29, 40. Bibliothèque des Arts Décoratifs Paris/Gianni Dagli Orti/The Art Archive: 17b.
Bibliothèque Nationale Paris/The Art Archive: front cover, 27, 32, 33. British Library London/The Art Archive: 12, 35, 37, 39.
Cabinet des Estampes Strasbourg/Gianni Dagli Orti/The Art Archive: 9. Canterbury Cathedral/Alfredo Dagli Orti/The Art Archive:
34. Mary Evans Picture Library: 18. Andrew Fox/Corbis: 14, 17t. Paul Hutley/Eye Ubiquitous/Corbis: 20. Jarrold Publishing/The Art
Archive: 38. JFB/The Art Archive: 21. Martin Jones/Corbis: 10. Private Collection/Marc Charmet /The Art Archive: 24.
Real Biblioteca de lo Escorial/Gianni Dagli Orti/The Art Archive: 5, 22. Statsbibliothek Nuremberg/Bridgeman Art Library: 31.
University Library Heidelberg/Gianni Dagli Orti/The Art Archive: 13.V & A Museum London/Eileen Tweedy/The Art Archive: 15.

9 8 7 6 5 4 3 2 1

CONTENTS

ALL ABOUT KNIGHTS

The medieval period of European history is from approximately 1000 to 1500. This was the era of the knights and a time of wars and crusades. In legend, knights are always brave fighters, jousting champions, and men of honor. But were real knights anything like the ones we imagine in films and stories? This book follows the imaginary life of a knight in the 1300s, but is based on true facts about the real knights of medieval Europe.

Feudal Society

Medieval society was feudal and made up of different people linked together by a network of agreements. The king, who owned all of the land, was the most powerful. The important nobles were given large areas of land by the king in return for service, which meant fighting for him when required. When the king needed them to fight, they had to bring along a number of men, including their knights. A noble could grant a knight a manor, an estate with some houses and land, in return for fighting a certain number of days a year. The knight swore fealty (loyalty) to his lord (the noble) and became his vassal, his sworn servant. The knight rented his land out to tenants (mostly peasants) who farmed the land and paid the knight with food or money.

Fighting Times

The rules of service for knights changed through the centuries. At first, they were expected to fight for their lord 40 days a year, for free. After the 40 days were up, they were paid. Later on, some knights became paid professionals as full-time fighters who rarely returned home. Knights could pay to avoid fighting, if they preferred, and were even allowed to pass on the cost of this to their tenants.

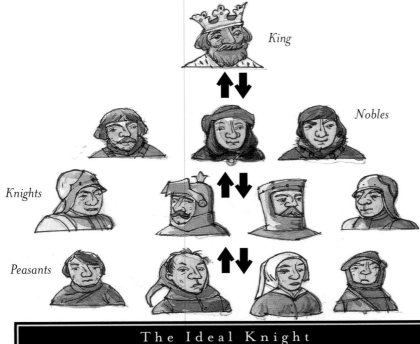

King

Nobles

Knights

Peasants

The Ideal Knight

The English poet Geoffrey Chaucer describes an ideal knight in his fourteenth-century book, *The Canterbury Tales*. This quote has been translated from the original into modern English:

❖ *There was a knight, a most distinguished man,*
Who from the day on which he first began
To ride abroad had followed chivalry,
Truth, honor, generousness and courtesy.
He had done nobly in his sovereign's war
And ridden into battle, no man more. ❖

During medieval times, knights were found in the four main kingdoms of Europe—France, Spain, England, and the Holy Roman Empire (including parts of central Europe, Germany, and Italy). Wales, Northern Ireland, and Scotland were not yet fully under English control.

Pictures such as this one from the 1800s have contributed to the romanticized—and inaccurate—ideas that people have about knights.

The Knight

This is the story of a knight who was born in 1319. He comes from a long line of knights, armed horsemen. His family originally came to England from Normandy, France, in 1066 with William the Conqueror's invading army. The family was given English land in return for fighting. Many English knights have French surnames. In the 1300s, there were approximately 6,000 knights in England.

A FUTURE KNIGHT IS BORN

The knight's family already has one son who, because he is the eldest male child, will one day inherit all of his father's land. The couple hope for a second son. However, he will have to claim land for himself when he is older by fighting well and impressing a noble. The lady of the manor will give birth to four boys and four girls but not all will survive past childhood.

Home Sweet Home

The manor house where the knight's family lives is similiar to a small castle with a gatehouse and walls around it. Inside the walls are a courtyard, kitchen block, stables, and a larger building that houses the Great Hall, the large main room. The Great Hall is where the knight

Some medieval manor houses, such as Ightham Mote in Kent, had a water-filled moat to protect the inhabitants from intruders.

meets visitors, the family eats, and the servants sleep in corners. Up above is the solar, which is the private family area.

There is a village on the manor lands and some of the village women have heard that the lady of the manor is in labor. They are now in the solar of the manor house to help at the birth. Soon the news of the birth of a baby boy is announced, and the villagers are pleased. Their lord, the knight, is good to them, but if he died without an heir, his estate could be given to a stranger. With two sons, this is less likely.

A Medieval Baby

The new baby is baptized on the day of his birth, given his name, and immersed in the chapel font three times. This is done as soon as he is born, in case he does not survive long. If he died unbaptized, the church believes he would not go to heaven. His mother does not feed him herself but finds him a wet nurse, a woman of the village who has recently given birth. She will breast-feed the baby for about 18 months, until he is strong. For now, he is swaddled (wrapped

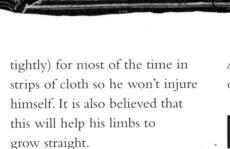

tightly) for most of the time in strips of cloth so he won't injure himself. It is also believed that this will help his limbs to grow straight.

The Retired Knight

The baby's father is in his late thirties. His fighting days as a knight are over, and he has retired to look after his estate. This includes the land his family has held for many years as well as the land that his wife's family gave them when they married. The baby's father owes fealty (fighting service) to the local lord, who has rights over this knight's family. The lord can tell the knight's children

A medieval baby, tightly wrapped, or swaddled, in strips of cloth.

Baptism

In 1302, Pope Boniface declares that humans can only go to heaven if they are Catholic.

❖ *It is necessary to salvation that every human creature be subject to the Roman pontiff.* ❖

who to marry, and, if their father dies when they are young, he might take all the money (such as rents) generated by the dead knight's lands, until the oldest child is old enough to inherit.

TIME TO LEAVE HOME

At the age of seven, the young boy is sent away from home to live in the household of another knight. He is going to spend the next few years being a "page." His parents choose a knight who lives in a manor similar to their own and not too far away. If they were important nobles, their son would have been sent to the king's court as a page.

A fourteenth-century page shows off his courtly manners in front of a group of noble ladies.

Learning from Ladies

The young page starts his new life under the direction of the ladies in his new home. They teach him courtly manners and social skills, such as dancing and reciting poetry. He learns something of music and the Bible. As a knight, he will be expected to cope well if he finds himself in someone's court with ladies to entertain. At dinner, he learns how to carve the meat and serve a meal to his lord. In this way, he is learning a lesson of allegiance, serving those above him.

Fighting and Writing

The young page also begins to learn the skills he will need to be a fighting knight. He goes hunting with the adults and learns to ride and shoot arrows accurately. He is lucky because there is a chaplain in the household. The priest teaches him some Latin and how to write using a feather quill on parchment made from goatskin. Most people in England cannot read or write, so this gives him an advantage.

While he is at the knight's house, he hears of trouble at the royal court. In 1327, news reaches them that Edward II has been murdered by his wife Isabella and her lover, Mortimer. In 1330, Edward II's son, Edward III, becomes old enough to take the throne. He imprisons Isabella and has Mortimer killed. These are uncertain times for knights who must stay friendly with those in power, so as not to lose their home and lands.

A page holds the bridle of a German knight's horse in this fourteenth-century painting.

A Busy Page

The page does not have a room of his own in the manor house; he sleeps in the Great Hall, in a warm corner near the fire. He is allowed to go home for holidays, birthdays, and special holy days. When he is not learning, he is kept busy with chores indoors and out. He must prepare the table for meals, light fires, work in the garden, and look after animals. This prepares him for a time when he might rule an estate of his own. He will have some understanding of how to run it and what work is needed.

BECOMING A SQUIRE

When he is 14, the page's parents watch their son receive a simple sword in a ceremony confirming him as a squire. He swears an oath of fealty, or loyalty, to the knight in whose household he lives. He is now expected to be that knight's personal servant in battle.

Serious Training

The young knight-to-be now begins his training in earnest. He learns to aim his lance at the quintain, a wooden arm with a shield on one side and a heavy sack on the other. If he fails to hit the shield full-on, the sack will swing around and knock him on the back of the head! He also practices aiming his lance through metal rings hanging in the trees.

He learns to ride superbly, controlling the horse with his knees and feet so that his hands are free to hold weapons. His saddle is shaped high at the front and back to help him stay on. He trains with two other squires and sometimes they have mock sword fights using wooden swords.

The Squire

Geoffrey Chaucer wrote a description of a squire in *The Canterbury Tales*, written in the fourteenth century. This version has been translated into modern English:

❖ *Short was his gown, the sleeves were long and wide;*
He knew the way to sit a horse and ride.
He could make songs and poems and recite,
Knew how to joust and dance, to draw and write. ❖

A modern version of a quintain. If the young squire misses the center of the shield, a heavy ball swings around and hits him.

Groups of squires sometimes behaved badly when they got together, occasionally getting out of control and having mass fights at events such as tournaments.

A manuscript painting depicts a smartly dressed squire showing off his riding skills.

Bodybuilding

The squire works at building up his strength so he will be strong enough to wear heavy chain-mail armor and mount a horse while wearing it. He tries to make himself stronger using a well-known squire's trick. He sews dirt into the pockets and hems of his clothing to make it heavier. He becomes good at vaulting over his horse while wearing chain mail, and he rides hard while hunting and leaping over ditches and hedges. He and the other squires are competitive and try to outdo each other in their knightly skills.

The Ideal Knight

As a squire, he learns about the code of chivalry. This a list of rules set out by the Catholic Church that explain what it means to be a good and noble knight. The ideal knight is supposed to protect the church, women and children, and the poor and the weak. On the battlefield, he is expected to play fair and accept the surrender of an enemy knight. He is not to kill an unarmed opponent. In reality, though, knights often behave poorly. Some are extremely violent and rob whomever they come across. The code is designed to try to keep the violent tendencies of knights in check.

A SQUIRE GOES FORTH

The squire acts as his lord's—his knight's—personal servant. He must go with him when he is called to do battle. In 1335, when the squire is 16, his lord's lord (the earl) calls upon his knights to help him put down a rebellion. The earl owes an obligation to the king to bring along knights, squires, archers, and men-at-arms (other troops, such as foot soldiers).

On the Journey

The squire sets out with one of his fellow squires to accompany the knight, their lord. They ride ahead, loaded down with baggage and leading extra horses. Before the trip, they clean the knight's armor in a barrel filled with vinegar and sand.

Along the way, the squires care for the horses and make sure all the equipment is safe. They act almost as butlers for the knight, folding his clothes, finding accommodations, and even tidying his hair. They help him put on his armor and mount his horse.

All Is Ready

Along the way, they are involved in a skirmish, a small-scale conflict with a band of rebels. The squire quickly hands over the knight's shield. Another young squire stays well behind the fighting, holding on to the extra horses. Before joining the fight, the knight makes the sign of the cross on his chest to ask for God's protection and mercy. Then he and his fellow knights ride toward the enemy, while the squires watch anxiously. If the rebels gain the advantage, the squires will have to fight for their lives.

A knight rides forth with his squire in attendance.

A Squire in Battle

If their knight is wounded during the fight, the squires must try to get him off the battlefield and out of danger. It is no easy job, as a knight's armor weighs him down, and the squires could be attacked by the enemy. Luckily for them, their knight is unharmed. This was a close-fought skirmish and, though the squire has trained nearly all his life for fighting, his first taste of a real fight is frightening. His experience of attending battles as a squire is designed to help him cope when he finally becomes a knight.

The squire's knight wears chain mail and carries a heavy sword in this modern depiction.

In this fifteenth-century painting, a procession of knights and squires, weary from travel, enter the safety of a castle.

BECOMING A KNIGHT

At the age of 18, the squire is judged ready to become a knight. He has already seen battle, and he proved brave and dependable. His lord is going to "dub" him—give him a knighthood in a special ceremony. Only a knight can dub another knight.

Preparing for the Ceremony

The squire's parents will attend the ceremony that is the most important day of their son's life so far. He prepares for it by fasting (not eating) for two days. His hair is cut short and he takes a bath to symbolically wash away his sins. Baths are an unusual occurrence—he usually washes with

water from a well. Before the day of the ceremony, he goes to the chapel and keeps a vigil, which means he prays to God through the entire night, his sword laid on the altar.

Dressing for the Part

On the special day, he is given ceremonial clothes to remind him of his religious duties as a knight. He is dressed in a white robe and belt to symbolize cleanliness. His red cloak is to remind him of his duty to shed blood in the defense of God. His brown stockings represent the earth he will one day return to when he dies. He is given shiny spurs to ensure he is swift at doing God's commands. The two edges of his sword represent justice and loyalty, and the crosspiece at the top symbolizes the holy cross.

A romanticized nineteenth-century picture of a squire keeping a vigil the night before his dubbing ceremony.

If a squire showed great bravery on the battlefield, he might be dubbed at that time. Not only was this a great honor but also much less expensive than a ceremony at home. A knight could only surrender to another knight during battle. So occasionally, if a squire took a knight prisoner, the enemy knight had to dub the squire on the spot, in order for the knight to surrender properly.

Arise, Knight!

The squire kneels before his lord, the knight, with his head bowed. The knight draws his own sword, holds it high above the squire's head and calls out his name. He makes a speech calling upon the squire to defend the weak, the poor, and the church and to obey his lord and king. Then he taps the squire on each shoulder with the flat of the sword. These are the only blows that the young man is expected to receive from now on without retaliating. He is now a knight.

Afterward there is a celebration feast. The ceremony is expensive for the new knight's family; their tenants will be asked to pay some of the cost of making this second son a knight. If the squire was from a grand family, the young man might have been knighted at court with other squires. This would have included a tournament and days of partying.

A king creates a new knight in this fourteenth-century manuscript painting.

ıcs an faıns poıv dawıstoılon.

INVITATION TO THE CASTLE

Now that he has been knighted, the young knight is invited to attend a jousting tournament at the Earl of Oxford's castle. Without the earl's goodwill, the young knight will never hold any land. He hopes to impress the earl and get a place in his service as a knight in his entourage, helping to guard the castle.

Hedingham Castle, the seat of the Earl of Oxford, is the most perfectly preserved Norman castle in the United Kingdom. This photo shows the keep, the strongest part of the castle.

The Castle Stronghold

The Earl of Oxford's castle is built with stone walls more than 11 feet (3.5 m) thick. Not only do the walls keep out the cold, but they make for a strong defense. The stronghold was first built in Norman times, when the family came over with William the Conquerer. The family name, de Vere, represents their French background. The great castle can be seen from the countryside and reminds the local people who is in charge. As the young knight approaches, he can see guards armed with arrows on the ramparts. There is a moat, a portcullis, and a drawbridge to let friends in but keep enemies out.

Castle Building

The chronicler Ordericus describes what happened to the unfortunate architect of Castle Ivri, in Normandy, during the late eleventh century:
❖ *This is the famous castle of great size and strongly fortified which was built by Alberede wife of Ralph, Count of Bayeux. It is said that Alberede, having completed this castle at vast expense, caused Lanfred, whose character as an architect transcended that of all other French architects of the time . . . to be beheaded that he might not erect a similar fortress anywhere else.* ❖

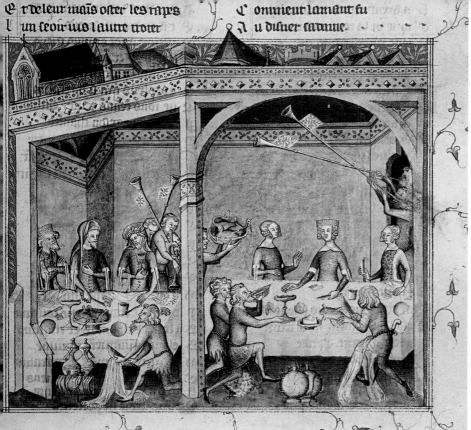

Medieval Facts

English nobles, such as earls and
barons, spoke a form of French
at this time, as their families
originated in France. It was a
mark of high class to speak
French.

*French people feasting in the fifteenth
century. Servants on bended knee present
drinking cups to the nobles.*

*At a feast, many courses are placed together
on the table at the same time, and musicians
play in the gallery.*

Inside the Walls

Within its walls, the castle has
several different buildings, such as
the stables, a chapel, workshops,
and kitchens. The knight enters
through the keep, an imposing tall
square building which is the heart
of the castle. He passes the
guardhouse on the ground floor
and goes through a corridor to the
Great Hall, where the earl receives
visitors. It is more magnificent than
any Great Hall he has seen before.
It has a giant stone arch, high
windows, and a fire blazing in a
huge hearth. Shields and stag
heads, the earl's hunting trophies,
hang from the walls. The earl's
family is very wealthy. They must
be in favor with the king, who
could easily take all of this away if
he so wished.

A Grand Feast

The new knight is invited to a
feast. Because he is a knight, he no
longer has to sit at the far end of
the hall with the squires. But he
feels ashamed as he is not wearing
new clothes—they are too
expensive for him. His armor, too,
is secondhand from his father and
not the latest style. He must start
to accumulate money of his own
by winning booty in war or by
winning prizes at tournaments so
that he can afford new clothes.

The feast is luxurious. The
servants serve many different
courses: dishes such as meat, fish,
baked eggs, and tarts. Spiced wine
and expensive sugar sweets are
also served.

JOUST!

The jousting tournament is the knight's opportunity to impress the earl with his fighting skills and perhaps win some prize money. The risk is that he will be injured. The contest is to be held in the castle meadows and will go on for a few days until a winner emerges. There is a sword-fighting contest on foot as well as the joust, but the young knight thinks his best chance is on horseback.

A lord and lady watch a joust in fifteenth-century France.

Rules of Jousting

When jousting first began, it was chaotic and very dangerous. By the 1300s, strict rules control what goes on. First, there is an official parade, and knights must register with the judges (only knights are allowed to take part). During a contest, two knights ride toward each other on horseback, each carrying a lance tipped with a breakable point called a coronel. Points are awarded for hitting either the center or the edge of a knight's shield, for breaking the point of a lance, and for unhorsing an opponent. After a few bouts between two knights, the scores are added up and the winner goes on to compete in the next round.

The Jousting Crowd

There are grandstands for the most important spectators, and the crowds have fun at sideshows and foodstalls. They cheer on their favorites. Some of the jousters are well-known professional jousting knights who travel from tournament to tournament, making a living by winning prizes. The ladies of the castle pick their favorite knights and give them favors to wear, such as a scarf or a circlet of flowers. No one has heard of the young knight, so he has everything to prove. He does well. At the feast after the tournament, the earl congratulates him on his skill. The young knight has made a very good start.

Knights had another sport, too. They sometimes took part in *combats a plaisance*, "combats for pleasure." For fun, one group of knights might try to defend a spot such as a bridge or a hill against another group of knights.

Jousting Dangers

The young knight is unharmed, but other knights are not so lucky. They break bones and need medical care. They might be given a painkiller, a syrup made from the henbane plant mixed with alcohol, while their limb is set. The most dangerous outcome is for a knight to get trapped as he falls and be dragged along by his galloping horse. That might lead to death or an incurable injury. Knights must hope that their wounds do not become infected, for that can lead to amputation or death.

Unfortunately, amputation is quite common after battles. A sharp sword is used to cut off the limb that is then bound up to stop the bleeding and cauterized (burnt) to try to seal it from infection. Sometimes wounds are stitched with a bone needle and thread made from animal intestines.

Some knights needed medical treatment after a tournament. A knight from Castille (now Spain), Don Pero Nino, received treatment for a wounded leg. The hot iron was used to seal his wound:

❖ *They heated an iron. . .white hot. The surgeon feared to apply it, having pity for the pain it would cause. But Pero Nino, who was used to such work, took the glowing iron and himself moved it over his leg, from one end of his wound to the other.* ❖

Lances shatter on shields as jousting knights collide.

CALLED TO WAR

Now that he is a knight in the Earl of Oxford's retinue (his personal guard), the young knight lives in the castle and is ready to guard it if necessary. When King Edward III calls upon the earl to help fight his enemy, the knight goes too, as one of the fighting men the earl is expected to provide for the king's army.

War Means Profit

War is a chance for a knight to make some money. If he captures a noble prisoner, he can demand a ransom from the family, before setting his hostage free. If he fights well, he might be awarded some land back home or even in a conquered country. Knights who have already inherited lands fight too, as part of their obligations to the earl. Knights can return home after their regulation 40 days of service, but this young knight stays on and is paid a wage by the earl. If his commanders allow it, he will take plunder from towns he helps to conquer. He will then send it home to be sold for cash.

During the Hundred Years' War, Edward the Black Prince (center right) takes King John II of France prisoner at the battle of Poitiers in 1356.

Medieval Facts

In 1192, the English King Richard I was captured in Austria and a "king's ransom" of 150,000 silver marks was demanded, worth billions in modern terms. Much of this money was raised by taxing the English people.

Pillage and Murder

The knight takes part in a tactic called the *chevauchée*. He raids enemy country, laying waste to crops and setting fire to farms and villages. The aim is to insult the knights whose land is ravaged, anger the foreign king, and draw the enemy army out to fight. Because the English army will go home in winter when conditions for fighting are too difficult, they want to get on with fighting as soon as they can. Food is seized to feed the invading army and peasants are murdered. It is a brutal tactic that is not in keeping with the idea of merciful and honorable knighthood told to young pages and ladies back home.

Knights at Sea

For the next few years, the knight accompanies the earl to sieges and skirmishes abroad. He travels by boat, along with his horses and equipment, returning home each winter after successful fighting. He is on the earl's ship when it is blown off course and is shipwrecked. The crew and passengers are lucky to survive, although the locals rob them of everything they have.

During a siege abroad, the king sends the earl home for more horses and supplies. The earl returns with 200 ships, but they meet the enemy fleet and are forced to fight them at sea. In a sea battle such as this, the opposing archers fight a duel of arrows and the knights draw their swords to fight the enemy on deck. The knight fights bravely and the earl's men win and capture enemy ships.

BATTLEFIELD TACTICS

The knight's commanders are the senior nobles in charge of the king's forces. They decide how battles are to be fought and sieges carried out. The king's son is a skilled commander. When he is present, he takes command and leads them to great victories.

Fighting in the Fourteenth Century

Before the knight's time, if a big battle was to be fought, knights lined up with the other knights on horseback in a closely packed row. When given the order, they would charge—thundering down on the enemy army. They pierced as many as they could with their lances before drawing their swords. But now the English are beginning to fight differently because their archers are becoming so skilled with longbows, a large form of bow and arrow. They can kill enemy knights from quite a distance. Now the English knights dismount and stand with the archers, beating off the oncoming enemy until the enemy forces are exhausted. The English knights then mount up and chase after the weakened enemy, cutting them down.

The Battle of Crécy

The knight has heard how, at the Battle of Crécy in 1346, the English positioned themselves on a ridge of higher ground to defend themselves against the French, who still fought in the traditional way. Despite the fact that the French forces far outnumbered the English, the French were in for a big shock.

The English knights stood with the archers. First, the French sent their crossbowmen forward, without their proper shields in place. (The shields had not arrived in time, but the French were impatient to fight.) The crossbowmen were being cut down by the archers. The mounted French knights could wait no longer and rode over their own unfortunate crossbowmen to attack the English. Wave after wave of French knights on horseback were slaughtered by the English longbowmen. Any who got through had to fight the English knights. It was a tremendous English victory.

Fighting on Foot

All the sword-fighting training comes into its own when the knight fights on foot. It is hard for him to move freely in his armor, but enemy knights are in the same position. He looks for a coat-of-arms (badge of identification) on the shields and surcoats (tunics) of other knights to determine who is an enemy and who is on his side. He has a big broad sword and needs both hands to wield it. His technique is to raise it high and drive it downward. If he thought he was losing, he would surrender and hope that he could raise his ransom, but this never happens to the knight, who is an outstanding fighter. Occasionally, he sees knights running away from battle, and this leaves them in disgrace. After the battle, foot soldiers pick up piles of armor and any weapons they want.

A fifteenth-century depiction of the Battle of Crécy showing English forces (left) about to cross the River Somme.

Battle of Crécy

Le Morte d'Arthur, a book about King Arthur written by Sir Thomas Malory in 1485, includes a long, detailed, and violent description of a medieval battle:

❖ *Then Brastias smote one of them on the helm, that it went to the teeth, and he rode to another, and smote him, that the arm flew into the field. Then he went to the third and smote him on the shoulder, that shoulder and arm flew in the field.* ❖

DRESSED TO KILL

By now, the knight has bought himself some up-to-date armor and a fine warhorse. Styles of armor change frequently through the years, but one thing does not change—it is very expensive. It is handmade and designed to keep out arrows and take sword blows without splitting. The knight can now afford to have it made specifically for him by a blacksmith.

This mounted knight has the fleur-de-lis *emblazoned on his shield and it is repeated on his horse's long coat, or caparison.*

All Kinds of Armor

The knight's armor consists of many different pieces. These include gauntlets, padded underclothes, and a number of protective armor plates held together with rivets and leather straps. He wears a chain mail coat, made from interlocking iron rings. It is called a hauberk and has a chain mail hood. Under the hood is a padded cap called a coif and over it a helmet with a visor. He also wears cloth stockings underneath chain mail stockings with leather soles. He wears a surcoat—a cloth tunic—over the top of the chain mail coat. The names of all these elements are derived from medieval French.

Heraldry

The knight's surcoat and his shield are marked with his coat-of-arms (so called because it is displayed on the surcoat). He has adapted his traditional family coat-of-arms, adding some new details for himself. Each knight has his own coat-of-arms, which is recorded by official heralds. Each coat-of-arms has its own specific colors, geometric design, and a symbol, such as an animal or an object. It might have stripes and a French motto. The earl has a coat-of-arms made up of red and yellow quarters with a white star in the top left quarter. Everyone recognizes it because the earl is a famous and successful fighting noble.

Warhorses

Like all knights, the young knight chooses warhorses that are fast and strong. These expensive horses are called destriers. The horses wear armor pieces and sometimes chain mail. They wear a long cloth coat called a caparison that is marked with the knight's coat-of-arms. Destriers are ridden only in battle; the knight has other horses for everyday riding. His destrier has been trained in mock battles and it knows how to charge, turn, and stop by obeying the pressure of the knight's knees and sharp spurs.

Knight in Shining Armor

A contemporary description of a knight's armor is included in the fourteenth-century tale, *Sir Gawain and the Green Knight*, by an unknown author. This is a modern translation:

❖ *He had polished armor on arms and elbows,*
Glinting and fine, and gloves of metal,
And all the goodly gear to give help, whatever befell him;
With surcoat richly wrought,
Gold spurs attached in pride,
A silken sword-belt athwart.
And steadfast blade at his side. ❖

Heavily armored mounted knights clash in this fourteenth-century manuscript illustration.

WEAPONS

The knight has trained to use a sword and a lance in battle. His expensive sword is made by a skilled craftsman. To lose it or to break it would be a costly misfortune. When he first became a knight, he was given one of his lord's swords as a gift. As his wealth has increased, he has had a finer, more decorated sword made for himself. He always has it blessed on a church altar before he uses it in battle.

A Fine Fighting Sword

The sword is made from steel heated and beaten into shape. While it is hot, the soft metal is folded over and over many times to make it stronger. The swords of rich nobles are embedded with precious jewels in the hilt. The knight's sword is not that grand, but it is engraved with beautiful patterns and fits into a finely decorated leather scabbard. He also has a dagger to use if he loses his sword in battle. The best dagger-fighting technique is to stab an opponent in the eye through the visor of his helmet or stab him through gaps in his armor.

Different Swords and Weapons

Sword shapes change regularly, and knights who come from abroad carry differently styled swords. Some swords are short and wide while others are long and tapered. All have a cross guard at the top to protect the knight's hand. Some knights fight with small axes rather than daggers. Foot soldiers have bigger axes with a jabbing spike.

Medieval weaponry including a sword, flail, lance, and axes.

The Knight's Tale

"The Knight's Tale," part of Geoffrey Chaucer's *The Canterbury Tales*, includes a description of a battle. This version has been translated into modern English:

❖ *Up spring the spears to twenty foot in height,*
Out go the long-swords flashing silver bright,
Hewing the helmets as they shear and shred.
Out bursts the blood in streams of sternest red,
The mighty maces swing, the bones are bashed. ❖

Time to Surrender

The knight's worst fear is to meet an enemy with a weapon that will break open his armor, such as a mace, flail, or hammer. A mace is a metal ball nailed onto a wooden shaft. A flail is a wooden shaft attached to a chain with an iron ball on the end. If a knight finds himself at the mercy of such a weapon, he knows the best thing to do is surrender.

A craftsman makes chain mail from interlocking iron rings. Medieval fighting gear was expensive because it was carefully handmade.

SIEGE WARFARE

The knight is involved in a few sieges that surround any town that refuses to surrender. Most towns have high walls and try to keep entrances protected by archers and fighting men. The townspeople inside hope to last until the enemy forces grow too tired and hungry to stay or decide to go home for winter.

Siege Equipment

Among the forces, there are craftsmen who know how to build special equipment to help break into a town or castle. Four-sided wooden siege towers, with giant ladders, help troops reach the tops of walls, though the men run the risk of being shot at from above. The knight has seen siege towers set on fire by flaming arrows. Giant catapult machines called trebuchets launch rocks to break down walls, and a battering ram can be used to try to break down doors. It is fitted with a sharp iron tip and mounted on wheels. The wooden roof protects its soldiers.

Digging or Bribing?

The commanders decide on the best strategies to try to make a breech—a hole in a defensive wall—where their troops can get through. One way to break into a town or castle is to dig a tunnel under its walls. As the men dig, they reinforce the tunnel walls with timbers. Once the tunnel is ready, the timbers are wrapped in pigskin and set on fire. When the timbers collapse, so does the tunnel, bringing down the wall above. However, digging takes a long time, and the townspeople look for signs of digging. They also might dig a tunnel going the other way and meet the enemy for an underground fight. The easiest way to break a siege is to bribe a traitor to open the gates from the inside.

This siege tower could be pushed up to castle walls to attack the defenders.

Medieval Facts

In 1203, knights entered the besieged Chateau Gaillard in France by crawling along the sewage trench. Once inside, the knights, disguised as locals, lowered the drawbridge.

Violence

The violent behavior of the English after their victory in 1370 at the siege of Limoges, a town in France, was chronicled by Froissart:

❖ *All who could be found were put to the sword, including many who were in no way to blame. I do not understand how they could not have failed to take pity on people who were too unimportant to have committed treason. . . . More than three thousand men, women and children were dragged out to have their throats cut.* ❖

Surrender or Die

If a besieged town or castle quickly surrenders, the people inside may be given quarter—mercy—by the victorious commanders. However, this is by no means certain, and the knight often sees troops running riot, with no one able to control them. Men, women, children, and priests may be put to the sword and any enemy knights hanged. Even if the violence is controlled by the commanders, the townspeople can expect anything of value to be taken. The troops move into people's homes, and a senior soldier is put in charge of the town. The knight plunders what he can and sends it home by boat to be sold.

English forces (left) storm the town of Caen in Normandy in 1346 – from an edition of Froissart's Chronicles.

PILGRIMAGE

At the age of 36, the knight feels he has had enough of fighting. He is no longer expected to go abroad with the earl because he is too old. He is free to retire to the estate he has been given by the earl for fighting bravely. But before he settles into country life, he wants to go on a pilgrimage.

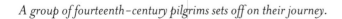

A group of fourteenth-century pilgrims sets off on their journey.

A Holy Journey

The knight travels to a holy shrine, a place connected to a saint who might hear his prayers and put in a good word for him in heaven. The journey is also the medieval version of a holiday. He chooses Canterbury and travels with his young squire and other pilgrims on a well-trodden route. By

Pilgrimage

In *The Canterbury Tales*, Geoffrey Chaucer describes a knight. Once a heroic fighter, he is done with battles and goes on a pilgrimage. This version has been translated into modern English:
❖ *Speaking of his equipment, he possessed Fine horses, but he was not gaily dressed. He wore a fustian tunic stained and dark, With smudges where his armor had left mark.* ❖

praying at Canterbury, pilgrims hope they will gain forgiveness for their sins. The knight also prays for the souls of those friends and family who died from the Black Death in the terrible years from 1348 to 1350. He is a survivor, but many people he knew from his father's estate and his own lands had died.

Fighting for Religion

The knight remembers tales of his ancestors who fought religious wars in the Holy Land (now called the Middle East). For 200 years after 1095, knights traveled to Jerusalem on crusades to recapture the holy city from Islamic control. Crusade battles and sieges were fierce and bloody (below). There were massacres and violent acts on both sides. From these crusades, a group of fighting monks called the Knights Templar emerged. Now the Knights Templar have been destroyed by European monarchs who thought they were too powerful.

Religion

Everyone is religious in medieval England. The knight hears a mass from a priest every day, and he always made a confession of his sins before battle, in case he died. By confessing his sins, he believes he will be forgiven by God. Medieval England is a Roman Catholic country, like the rest of Europe at this time. The pope is the religious leader, and he tries to get the monarchs to do what he regards as best for the church. The pope would like knights to go on crusades again, but it is too expensive and there are battles to fight nearer home, so crusading is no longer a popular idea.

This depiction (right) of a praying crusader is from a twelfth-century manuscript.

The knight returns to his estate; his fighting days are over. His parents and the lord who trained him to be a knight have all died. His older brother inherited the original family estate and paid the earl an expensive "relief," or tax, to be allowed to do so. Because of this, the knight does not have to pay death duties.

The Knight's Wife

The knight married in his twenties, during a break between fighting seasons. He married quite late in life because he had no lands when he was young and was not a good prospect for a bride. By contrast, his older brother was betrothed (promised) as a seven-year-old child to another young child. The two married when he was 14 and she was 12.

The earl chose a wife for the knight—the daughter of another one of his loyal knights.

Hunting with hawks was a sport enjoyed by many knights.

The couple had no choice in the matter; they had to do what the earl wished or risk his displeasure. The lady has looked after the knight's land and manor every time he has gone away to fight. She has also given birth to four children—only a son and a daughter have survived past the age of five. Sadly, the others died of infections and diseases when they were babies. The knight now returns home for good and takes over running the estates.

The Daily Round

The knight employs some servants to help him run his estate. He also has a steward to help him sort out household matters and a reeve to help him collect taxes due to him from the peasants. Every morning, he makes the rounds by riding around the estate with his steward and checking up on the state of the farmland and the woods.

Peasants cut corn while the reeve supervises, from a fourteenth-century psalter.

He visits the mill, which he owns and rents to the miller. The miller grinds the corn grown by the local peasants, and the knight takes a daily percentage of the flour produced. It is the knight's duty to check on the mill and on any shops he owns and rents out, such as the baker's. He wants to be sure the shops are clean and well run. Otherwise, angry locals will begin complaining to him.

Pleasures of the Day

Most knights love to hunt, and it is a way of feeding the people who live in the manor house. The knight has hunting dogs and keeps trained hawks and falcons to hunt rabbits and small birds. He uses a bow and arrow to shoot deer and wild pigs in his woodlands. As the day draws to a close, he spends time in his private quarters with his family, telling his children tales of his fighting days. Sometimes traveling entertainers visit—jugglers or a wandering minstrel who sings songs of knightly legends and magical happenings.

Love of Hunting

The following quote is from the *Livre de Chasse*, by nobleman Gaston de Foix. It is a famous book on medieval hunting. Gaston died after a day out hunting in 1391.

❖ *All my life I have delighted especially in three things: one is arms, a second is love, and third is the chase.* ❖

KNIGHTLY DUTIES

A t home, the knight is the local judge as well as the tax collector. He decides on disputes and determines punishments. The tenants look to him to behave honorably and fairly. He also has a duty to offer the tenants protection from any possible attack, and he trains the men in case they need to fight.

Medieval justice — the stocks pinned an offender's legs while villagers threw rubbish at them.

Knightly Justice

The knight regularly holds court sessions in his Great Hall, where people present complaints against others. These vary from accusations of cheating or stealing to more serious charges such as rape or murder. The most common grievances the knight deals with are disputes between neighbors over land, animals, or poaching; shopkeepers cheating customers; or someone complaining of a grave insult. He must judge these and levy fines or physical punishment such as receiving lashes, being placed in the village stocks, or hanging for a serious crime. Sometimes a jury helps him decide on judgments.

Collecting Taxes

Every person who lives on the knight's land has an obligation (duty) to pay a "quota," whether it be goods or money, to the knight. A farmer might pay in food, a shopkeeper in goods. A lowly peasant might work the lord's farmland for a few days, and a peasant's wife might be sent to help out in the manor house. The knight sends his reeve to collect taxes. The reeve takes a percentage of what he collects. Someone who fails to pay could be fined, physically punished, or even face eviction.

Training the Locals

If the knight's lands are ever attacked, his tenants will expect him to give them shelter in his manor house. He also trains the men to fight if needed. Every Sunday after church, they gather in a meadow to practice their archery. Sometimes he runs contests with prizes to keep them interested and enthusiastic. He might hang up a straw dummy or mount a target on wheels and roll it along to see if his tenants can hit it as it moves.

If the knight's manor was attacked, he was duty-bound to shelter peasants such as this one depicted in the Luttrell Psalter *ca. 1340.*

DEATH OF A KNIGHT

In 1360, the Earl of Oxford died. The knight visited his castle to pay his respects to the old earl's nephew, the new earl. The knight is feeling his age. He has seen great dangers, including the death of a third of the English population by the Black Death. Mercifully, he survived and finally dies peacefully in 1379, at the age of 60. This is not an unusual lifespan for someone of his rank and background. Peasants die much younger, because of poor diet and living conditions.

Knights line up to pledge fealty (allegiance) to a new overlord, in this case a king.

A Knight's Tomb

Inside the local church, the knight is laid to rest in a stone sepulchre (a stone box above the ground). On top of the tomb, an effigy is carved in the current style—a stone sculpture represents the knight in his armor. He is depicted as relaxed and his legs are crossed. One hand is on his sword, and his feet rest on a carved lion. The tomb is carved with his coat-of-arms and some "weepers." These small figures might represent mourning family members, angels, or saints. The tomb is a reminder to everyone of the knight's bravery and the importance of his family.

Medieval Facts

In the 1300s, gunpowder and cannons were brought to Europe from China. The English first used a cannon against the French at the Siege of Calais in 1346.

To Avalon

Sir Thomas Malory, a knight, wrote *Le Morte d'Arthur* in 1470. The last words of the dying King Arthur, as he drifts away on a magical boat to the blessed Isle of Avalon, are:

❖ *I will into the vale of Avalon to heal me of my grievous wound; and if thou hear no more of me, pray for my soul.* ❖

A knight's funeral could be a grand but solemn affair.

A New Coat-of-Arms

The knight's family is fortunate. One of his sons has survived and inherits his lands and title. His son uses the family coat-of-arms but adds a new symbol of his own. The knight's daughter can combine the coat-of-arms with her husband's coat-of-arms when she marries. If the knight had left no sons, his inheritance could have gone to his daughter if the earl allowed it. The family continues to owe allegiance to the earl, just as their father did before them.

The End of the Fighting Knights

The age of the fighting knights will soon end. A line of charging knights is no match for a line of powerful long-range longbows or the cannon which will be used more and more in battle. By 1500, the knight's descendants will no longer fight for their lord. Instead, the king will use a professional army, and the knights will become local gentry concentrating on managing their estates. But the legends surrounding the knights of medieval times will survive for many centuries to come. When the knight was young, he was inspired by tales of King Arthur's knights. Those myths will still be told hundreds of years later, keeping the idea of the chivalrous knight alive.

GLOSSARY

Archer ❖ a soldier trained to fire arrows from a bow

Betrothal ❖ a marriage arrangement, in which young people are promised to each other in marriage

Black Death ❖ the name given to the disease that ravaged Europe in the late 1340s

Breech ❖ a hole smashed in the wall of a castle by a besieging enemy

Caparison ❖ a cloth coat worn by a medieval warhorse

Chain mail ❖ armor made from interlocking metal rings

Chevauchée ❖ a rampage by a medieval army through enemy country to devastate farms and crops and kill people

Chivalry ❖ a code of honorable behavior for knights

Coat-of-arms ❖ the official badge of a noble family

Cross guard ❖ a piece of steel between the handle and the blade of a sword

Crusades ❖ a series of religious wars fought in medieval times between Christian and Islamic forces for control of Jerusalem, the city that is revered as holy in both religions

Destrier ❖ a medieval warhorse

Dubbing ❖ the ceremony of a knight making someone else a knight by tapping their shoulders with a sword

Fealty ❖ loyalty or allegiance to someone, sealed with an oath

Flail ❖ a metal ball on the end of a chain fixed to a wooden shaft used as a weapon for crushing armor

Gatehouse ❖ the entrance to property such as a manor or a castle

Great Hall ❖ the large main room in a castle or manor where meetings were held and meals eaten

Heir ❖ someone who is first in line to inherit land, goods, and perhaps a noble title passed down to them on their parents' death

Heraldry ❖ the official record of different coats-of-arms (badges identifying different noble families)

Holy Roman Empire ❖ a medieval kingdom stretching over central Europe, Germany, and Italy

Inheritance ❖ land, money, and sometimes a noble title handed on by a relative when they die—the oldest son was always first in line to inherit everything

Joust ❖ a tournament where two knights rode towards each other and scored points by striking their opponent with a lance

Knights Templar ❖ a group of religious knights who fought in the crusades during the twelfth century

Lance ❖ a long metal pole with a sharp point, fixed to a wooden shaft

Mace ❖ a metal ball nailed to a wooden shaft and used as a weapon

Money ❖ pounds (£), shillings, and pennies, or pence, were the main coins used in Britain in medieval times. A mark was a coin worth 13 shillings, 4 pence

Norman ❖ something or someone connected to the French forces that invaded England in 1066, led by William the Conquerer from Normandy; a castle described as Norman means it was built by the French invaders

Page ❖ a young boy, age seven or more, who served a knight and his family while learning to be a knight

Pilgrimage ❖ a trip to a holy shrine

Plunder ❖ stealing goods and money from conquered people during an invasion

Portcullis ❖ the fortified entrance gate of a castle that slid up and down

Pounds ❖ *see money*

Quarter ❖ mercy given to conquered soldiers by a victorious force—(to "give no quarter" means to give no mercy)

Quintain ❖ a wooden training aid used for improving a knight's aim with a lance; it had a shield on one side and a heavy sack on the other side which would hit a knight if he missed the shield

Ramparts ❖ the walkways around the tops of castle walls

Ransom ❖ a sum of money paid to release a hostage from captivity

Reeve ❖ a knight's personal tax collector

Relic ❖ a religious object connected to a saint

Retinue ❖ a group of knights who personally guarded a noble

Scabbard ❖ a sword holder made out of leather in medieval times

Shillings ❖ *see money*

Siege tower ❖ a wooden tower with ladders on each side that rolled up to the wall of a castle for invading soldiers to climb up

Skirmish ❖ a fight between two enemy groups; smaller than a full-scale battle

Solar ❖ a private family room above the Great Hall in a castle or manor

Squire ❖ a young man (age 14) who served a knight and was training to be a knight

Steward ❖ a knight's household assistant who helped him manage his estate

Surcoat ❖ a tunic worn by a knight on top of his armor

Swaddling ❖ strips of cloth tightly wrapped around a medieval baby

Tenant ❖ someone who rents land or property belonging to someone else

Trebuchet ❖ a giant wooden catapult used to launch rocks at a castle during a siege

Vigil ❖ a long session of prayer that lasts for many hours; a squire held a vigil the night before he became a knight

Wet nurse ❖ a woman paid to breast-feed another woman's baby

Useful Medieval History Web Sites

http://library.thinkquest.
org/10949/fief/
medknight.html
This Web site describes
how a boy became a knight
and includes pictures and
information regarding the
clothing, weapons,
tournaments, and the
concept of chivalry.

http://www.medieval-
life.net/chivalry.htm
This Web site provides
information on medieval
life, knights, and literature.

www.mnsu.edu/emuseum
/history/middleages/
contents.html
Enter this Web site and
choose a guide (knight,
merchant, nun, or peasant)
or topic and learn more
about medieval life.

TIME LINE

ca.1000	Europe experiences a great expansion in its population.
1000	Tournaments occur for the first time in England.
1050	Knights begin to charge with lances.
1066	William of Normandy invades England and is crowned king in December.
1096	The First Crusade begins.
ca. 1100	Over the next 200 years, there is a great expansion of peasant settlement in Europe.
ca. 1100	There is a gradual introduction of the "three-field" agricultural system across much of northern Europe.
1135–1154	Civil war breaks out in England.
1146–1254	The Second through Seventh Crusades occur.
1150	Knights begin to use coats-of-arms.
1200	Knights begin protecting their horses with armor.
ca. 1200	Some peasant houses are being built of stone in northern Europe.
ca. 1200	In northern Europe, horses replace cattle to pull heavy loads.
ca. 1200	Money rents replace labor services across Europe. There is a growth in towns, trade, and the economy. There is an increase in the supply of coins and a demand for luxury goods.
1205	The River Thames freezes and can be crossed over the ice.
1207	The Order of St. Francis is formed in Italy.
1208	King John quarrels with the pope who bans church services in England.
1215	King John signs the Magna Carta that gives the nobles more power.
1252	Henry III is given a polar bear, which swims in the River Thames with a muzzle and chain.
1260	The cathedral is consecrated in Chartres, France.
1265	Marco Polo travels to the Far East.
ca. 1270	The oldest paper manufacturing in Christian Europe is in Fabriano, Italy.
1279	England introduces new silver coins.
1285	Spectacles are made in northern Italy.
ca. 1310	The mechanical clock is perfected.
1317	Europe experiences heavy rain and ruined harvests; famine spreads across Europe.
1327	Edward II is murdered.
1323–1328	The peasants revolt in the Netherlands.
1337	The Hundred Years' War between England and France begins.
1344	The English make their first gold coin.
1346	At the Battle of Crécy, an early cannon and longbows are used.
1348–1349	The bubonic plague (Black Death) spreads through Europe.
1361	Europe experiences another outbreak of the plague.
1362	William Langland writes his poem *Piers Plowman*.
1369	Harvests fail across Europe.
1381	The Peasant Revolt occurs in England.
1387	Chaucer begins writing *The Canterbury Tales*.
1388	The first town sanitation act is passed in the English parliament.
1430–1470	England experiences economic crises—many peasants are ruined.
1437–1438	Many parts of Europe experience the plague, ruined harvests, and famine.
1438–1440	England experiences heavy rain and ruined harvests.
1453	The Hundred Years' War between England and France ends.
1470	An economic revival begins.
1500	Knights no longer go to war—now their role is to be landowners.

INDEX

These are the lists of contents for each title in *Medieval Lives*: